The Facts on Famous Artifacts

THE TRAVELING MUMMY OF KING TUT

Dwayne Hicks

CREATED BY Humans

Published in 2027 by The Rosen Publishing Group, Inc.
2544 Clinton Street, Buffalo, NY 14224

First Edition

Editor: Greg Roza
Designer: Michael Flynn

Photo Credits: Cover, p. 5 LukeandKarla.Travel/Shutterstock.com; (series background) Yuliya Chsherbakova/Shutterstock.com; p. 7 Maciek67/Shutterstock.com; p. 9 https://commons.wikimedia.org/wiki/File:Tutankhamun_Los_Angeles_2018.jpg; p. 10 CK-TravelPhotos/Shutterstock.com; p. 11 https://commons.wikimedia.org/wiki/File:King_Tutankhamun%27s_tomb_goods_shield_with_image_of_the_King_threatening_lions_DSC_0944_(30769015407).jpg; p. 13 SinanDogan34/Shutterstock.com; p. 14 Jaroslav Moravcik/Shutterstock.com; p. 15 Michael Gordon/Shutterstock.com; p. 17 hemro/Shutterstock.com; p. 18 https://commons.wikimedia.org/wiki/File:Howard_Carter,_5-8-24_LOC_npcc.11276.tif?page=1; p. 19 https://commons.wikimedia.org/wiki/File:The_unbroken_seal_on_Tutankhamun's_tomb,_1922.jpg; p. 21 Everett Collection/Shutterstock.com; p. 22 Jaroslav Moravcik/Shutterstock.com; p. 23 https://commons.wikimedia.org/wiki/File:Tuts_Tomb_Opened.JPG; p. 25 https://commons.wikimedia.org/wiki/File:King_Tutankhamun%27s_tomb_goods_chair_DSC_0915_(43891821850).jpg; p. 27 b-hide the scene; p. 28 ZDL/Shutterstock.com.

Cataloging-in-Publication Data

Names: Hicks, Dwayne.
Title: The traveling mummy of King Tut / Dwayne Hicks.
Description: Buffalo, New York : Created by Humans, an imprint of Rosen Publishing, 2027. | Series: The facts on famous artifacts | Includes glossary and index.
Identifiers: ISBN 9781534553316 (pbk.) | ISBN 9781534553323 (library bound) | ISBN 9781534553330 (ebook)
Subjects: LCSH: Tutankhamen, King of Egypt--Tomb--Juvenile literature. | Mummies--Juvenile literature. | Excavations (Archaeology)--Juvenile literature.
Classification: LCC GN293.H53 2027 | DDC 932.014--dc23

Manufactured in the United States of America

CPSIA Compliance Information: Batch #CSCBH27. For Further Information contact Rosen Publishing at 1-800-237-9932.

CONTENTS

THE BOY KING

Chances are you've heard of King "Tut." He's the most famous mummy in the world! Tutankhamun became **pharaoh** of ancient Egypt more than 3,300 years ago. He was only about 8 or 9 at the time.

King Tut and his resting place in Egypt's Valley of the Kings have intrigued people since they were rediscovered by English archaeologist Howard Carter in the 1920s. Other archaeologists had stopped exploring the Valley of the Kings, but Carter believed there were still tombs to find. How did King Tut's tomb remain hidden for so long, especially when many other tombs had already been uncovered? Let's find out!

King Tut's mummy is an artifact! This is because it took many talented experts to prepare the body for burial. The decorations found with and on his body are also artifacts, but some are considered works of art as well.

The Valley of the Kings

The Valley of the Kings—located on the west bank of the Nile River near Luxor, Egypt—is a necropolis, or a burial ground for pharaohs and other officials. It was used from about 1540 to 1075 BCE. Tombs were cut into the rock cliffs of a dry riverbed. Archaeologists have uncovered about 70 tombs. Although the Valley of the Kings in is a dry riverbed, flash floods sometimes fill the empty tombs with water and debris.

FATHER AND SON

The pharaoh Akhenaten (c. 1353–1336 BCE) was a leader who shook up ancient Egypt by establishing a monotheistic religion honoring the sun god Aten. He blocked the worship of many other gods. This disrupted centuries of polytheistic tradition! Akhenaten also introduced new artistic and **architectural** styles to Egypt.

Akhenaten's reign resulted in economic difficulties and revolts in Egypt. He chose to ignore events outside of Egypt, including pleas for help from friendly neighboring states. He moved the capital form Thebes to Amarna. He became known as the **Heretic** Pharaoh. After Akhenaten's death, Egypt quickly returned to the traditional, polytheistic religion.

ARTI-FACT!

Polytheism is the belief in many gods and goddesses. Monotheism is the belief in one god. Some historians think Akhenaten was the world's first monotheist leader, but others believe he just preferred one god out of many.

This sculpture of Akhenaten shows the different artistic style he introduced during his reign. He felt art should be more realistic and less symbolic.

Akhenaten died in 1336 BCE. His son, Tutankhaten (born around 1342 BCE), took over as pharaoh when he was about nine years old. Two advisors governed Egypt at first, and they returned Egypt to its former state using Tutankhaten as a symbol of rebuilding. Tutankhaten's first official act was to change his name to Tutankhamun, which honors the god Amun. By recognizing traditional Egyptian gods, Tutankhamun showed that he wanted Egypt to return to it's old customs.

This was the beginning of the reign of King Tut! He was instantly popular, despite his young age, as his reign marked a return to order.

ARTI-FACT!

The name Akhenaten means "beneficial for Aten." Tutankhaten means "living image of Aten." The name Tutankhamun means "living image of Amun."

This statue of a young King Tut was found in his tomb when it was uncovered in 1922. Here, it is on display in Los Angeles, California.

King Tut was not a healthy person. This was likely a result of royal inbreeding. He was often frail and had several physical problems, including a lame left foot and a **cleft palate**. However, most artistic representations of him show him as a strong, capable leader, even in battle.

Tutankhamun married his half-sister Ankhesenamun, who had some influence on his reign. Ankhesenamun gave birth to two girls who did not live long. Their tiny mummified remains were found in King Tut's tomb. When Tutankhamun died around 1323 BCE with no heir to take the throne, Egypt was left in a period of uncertainty.

This is one of the shields removed from King Tut's tomb when it was rediscovered in 1922. It shows the pharaoh catching a lion with his bare hand. Do you think this is a realistic depiction of the boy king?

What Is Royal Inbreeding?

"Inbreeding" means having children with a close relative. Science has proven that this often results in physical and mental health problems. Royal inbreeding was once common in ruling families. It was thought that bloodlines were a direct path to divine leadership, or leadership ordained by a god or gods. Generations of royalty may be the product of inbreeding, increasing the chances of health problems. Other examples of this over the centuries include the Habsburgs of Spain and the Romanovs of Russia.

HOW DID TUT DIE?

Tutankhamun died in 1323 BCE at the age of 19, but we're not sure how he died. The remains of the pharaoh provide some interesting clues. There is a hole in the back of Tutankhamun's head. Some historians believe that he was **assassinated** or died in a **chariot** accident, but recent studies suggest that the hole was made during mummification.

Other studies have shown that Tutankhamun had an infected and broken leg when he died. Tests of King Tut's **DNA** revealed proof of **malaria** infections and bone disease. Tut's family background may also have resulted in illnesses leading to his death.

We may never discover the actual reason behind King Tut's death.

MUMMIFIED!

The ancient process of mummification was an Egyptian religious tradition for royalty and some other important figures. It required a special team of priests trained in **embalming**. The process took 70 days and included numerous rituals.

The priests had knowledge of human **anatomy**. They removed nearly all the organ's, wrapped them in specially prepared bandages, and placed them in clay containers called canopic jars. Only the heart remined in place. They removed all moisture from the body and wrapped it in hundreds of yards of linen. Amulets with religious words or phrases were wrapped in the linen as well. Often, a mask was placed over the mummy's face.

During the Middle Ages, people began to believe that mummies held magical properties. Many Europeans returned from Egypt with mummies. They were often ground into a powder to be used crop fertilizer and medicines. This process continued up until the early 1900s.

Packing Tut Away

After the process described on the previous page, priests placed a 24-pound (10.9 kg), solid-gold mask over Tut's head and shoulders. His body was wrapped tightly with long strips of linen. Strong bands with religious phrases were placed over the wrappings. The mummy was placed in a series of nested containers that included three golden coffins, a granite coffin, and four gold-covered wooden containers. This system of containers was so big it barely fit in the tomb, or burial chamber.

IN THE VALLEY OF THE KINGS

Tutankhamun's tomb is located in the Valley of the Kings. This is a royal necropolis near the banks of the Nile River. It is made up of several chambers. When rediscovered in the early 1900s, the entrance chamber had been looted, or stolen from, but the rest of the tomb had remained untouched over the centuries.

The outer chambers were crammed with more than 5,000 artifacts! This included chariots, weapons, shields, statues, furniture, clothes, jewelry, and more. Archaeologists found 130 walking sticks used by the pharaoh during his life. These were royal items that Tutankhamun would need in the afterlife.

Historians think Tutankhamun must have died suddenly because his burial chamber is small, especially for a pharaoh.

Remaining a Secret

The Valley of the Kings is home to more than 60 tombs for pharaohs and high-ranking officials. The location was selected in the hope of hiding it from looters. However, nearly all of the tombs have been looted. King Tut's tomb had been buried beneath rubble because of his connection to Akhenaten. In time, worker huts were built over the tomb. This allowed Tut's treasures to remain hidden for centuries.

DISCOVERY OF THE CENTURY

By the 1920s, archaeologists had thoroughly explored the tombs of the Valley of the Kings. British archaeologist, Howard Carter, had been uncovering Egyptian artifacts for 30 years. In 1922, while most archaeologists had given up, Carter made the discovery of the century.

HOWARD CARTER

This photograph shows the unbroken seal Carter found when he uncovered Tut's tomb.

Locating Tut's tomb, full of artifacts, helped archaeologist to understand more about Egyptian burials and culture. They now knew what a pharaoh's tomb looked like before being looted. While the outer chamber had been emptied years ago, Carter found a seal on the doors to the inner chambers. This meant the original tomb had not been disturbed for over 3,300 years.

Carter and his team spent a decade cataloging the artifacts found in the tomb. Most of the artifacts were sent to the Egyptian Museum in Cairo.

The walls of the tomb were painted with scenes depicting King Tut's journey to the afterlife. Several rooms branched off the burial chamber. The antechamber was packed with artifacts, including chariots that had been taken apart and stacked over furniture. A small room called the annex held jars of wine and oil, food containers, board games, and more. Items that ancient Egyptians found more valuable or religiously meaningful were stored in an room called the treasury.

Carter found Tut's inner chambers piled high with artifacts. The unorganized artifacts are another clue that the pharaoh died suddenly and was buried quickly.

UNBOXING KING TUT

Between early 1924 and late 1925, Carter and his team—under the watchful eyes of Egyptian officials—carefully removed the nested coffins. The innermost container was opened on October 28, 1925, finally revealing King Tut's mummy.

The mummy was covered in symbolic ornaments, including a dazzling gold burial mask. These proved hard to remove after sitting in the tomb for centuries. The outermost wrappings were inscribed with quotes supposedly from the gods. Removing the wrappings revealed the preserved remains of the ancient pharaoh.

This photograph shows Carter and a foreman inspecting the recently opened coffin of Tutankhamun.

The Burial Mask

King Tut's burial mask is a work of art. Two layers of high-quality gold were hammered into shape by talented craftsmen. The gold is inlaid with beautiful stones, including **lapis lazuli** and **obsidian**. The gold is inscribed with magic spells meant to keep the pharaoh's body safe. The mask has many important symbols on it, including the beard and the cobra on its forehead.

U.S. TOUR

In 1972, many of Tut's treasures were sent to the British Museum in London, England, for display. Soon after, U.S. officials met with Egyptian officials to arrange a showing in the Unites States. The "Treasures of Tutankhamun" took Tut's belongings to Washington, D.C., Chicago, New Orleans, Los Angeles, Seattle, and finally New York City.

About eight million Americans paid to see the show! Visitors followed a path that highlighted the actions of Howard Carter as he explored the tomb. It included about 50 artifacts, and the centerpiece was Tut's burial mask. The tour then went to Russia where it appeared in three cities.

ARTI-FACT!

In New Orleans, 870,594 people paid for tickets to the show, raising $75 million. When the show ended, they had a traditional New Orleans jazz funeral for the boy pharaoh!

The U.S. tour lasted from 1976 to 1979. It made millions of dollars, some of which went to the Cairo Museum for much needed repairs and updates.

HOME SWEET HOME

Tutankhamun's belongings have made other world tours over the years. Tours came to the United States between 2005 and 2011 and between 2009 and 2013. A tour that began in 2018 was cut short due to the Covid-19 pandemic.

Today, Tut's most fragile belongings, including the burial mask, remain at the Grand Egyptian Museum in Giza, Egypt. Tut's mummy is on display in his tomb in the Valley of the Kings. In fact, the boy pharaoh never strayed far from his original resting place! Visitors to the tomb can also view the wall of Tut's burial chamber with scenes of Tut in the afterlife.

ARTI-FACT!

Although Tut and his belonging don't travel much, several tours have brought hundreds of **replicas** to cities around the world. The newest tour includes a **virtual-reality** room where visitors are transported back to ancient Egypt!

King Tut rests in a climate-controlled glass case to keep his body from decaying.

EGYPTOLOGY

Tutankhamun's rediscovery in the 1920s helped popularize Egyptology, or the scientific study of ancient Egypt. This was a relatively new movement at the time. Archaeologists, historians, writers, artists, and even regular people became fascinated with the mysteries of ancient Egypt.

King Tut's burial mask has become a common image in popular culture. It has appeared on T-shirts, coffee mugs, and much more. It has even been used to sell products. King Tut, his mask, and his many royal artifacts will continue to amaze and inspire people for generations to come.

TIMELINE

c. 1353–1336 BCE	The reign of Akhenaten
c. 1342 BCE	Tutankhamun is born as Tutankhaten.
c. 1336 BCE	King Tut's reign begins.
c. 1334 BCE	King Tut restores Egyptian customs and gods. He moves the capital back to Thebes.
c. 1323 BCE	King Tut dies.
1914 CE	Howard Carter receives permission to dig in the Valley of the Kings.
November 4, 1922	Carter finds the entrance to King Tut's tomb.
1925	Carter opens King Tut's innermost coffin, reveling Tut's mummy and burial mask.
1976–1979	The "Treasures of Tutankhamun" tours the United States.
2005	Egyptian scientists discover that the hole in King Tut's head was made during the embalming process.

GLOSSARY

anatomy: The structural makeup of an organism.
architectural: Related to the design and construction of architecture, or buildings.
assassinate: To kill someone, often for political reasons.
chariot: An ancient two-wheel cart pulled by horses that was often used in war.
cleft palate: A split in the roof of the mouth that occurs as a birth defect.
DNA: A substance that carries genetic information in a plant or animal's cells.
embalm: To treat a dead body with special preparations to preserve it from decay.
heretic: Someone who believes or teaches something that goes against accepted or official beliefs.
lapis lazuli: A deep blue stone that is used in jewelry.
malaria: A serious disease with chills and fever that's spread by the bite of a mosquito.
obsidian: A black, glassy rock formed by quickly cooling lava.
pharaoh: A king or ruler of ancient Egypt.
replica: An exact or very close copy of something.
virtual reality: An artificial environment that is experienced through sights and sounds provided by a computer and in which one's actions partly decide what happens in the environment.

FOR MORE INFORMATION

BOOKS

Bearce, Stephanie. *Awesome, Disgusting, Unusual Facts About Mummies*. Minneapolis, MN: Black Rabbit Books, 2024.

Jackson, Tom. *The Pharaoh's Revenge: King Tut and Other Mummy Curses.* North Mankato, MN: Lerner Publishing, 2026.

WEBSITES

Ancient Egypt for Kids
www.ducksters.com/history/ancient_egypt.php
Read about ancient Egypt and find links to related topics.

Mummy Mystery: King Tut
kids.nationalgeographic.com/history/article/king-tut
Learn more fascinating facts about King Tut and see more images of his burial tomb and the artifacts discovered there.

INDEX